Start Smart Launch Roadmap

Juliana A. Taylor

Copyright © 2013 Juliana A. Taylor

All rights reserved.

ISBN: 1494238616
ISBN-13: 978-1494238612

DEDICATION

This book is dedicated to everyone who contributed to the successful launch of Start Smart. After three years of developing our brand, building our network and developing an understanding of our market, we've officially launched. We look forward to building on the progress we've made so far, and having an even greater impact on the lives of entrepreneurs around the world.

Dear Reader,

It's a pleasure to share the *Start Smart Launch Roadmap* with you. In many ways this book is an account of the lessons we've learned and challenges we've faced while launching Start Smart. We sincerely hope that by sharing our experiences, you will emerge with the tools necessary to successfully launch your business, product or service.

As with our other resources, by purchasing our book, you have already begun to apply two of the most important concepts in the world of entrepreneurship:

Learning. As an entrepreneur it is essential to continuously learn and build knowledge on your industry, customers, competition and product(s).

Planning. Do not let the world take you by surprise. Small business owners in particular tend to be more heavily impacted by changes in their business environment. This is because their market is often narrower and their resources more limited. It is therefore important to do your best to plan ahead, so that when the unexpected does arise, you will be able to do something about it.

To learn more about us and how we can help your business, visit www.startsmartgh.com.

Happy reading!

Best Wishes
Juliana A. Taylor & the Start Smart Team

CONTENTS

1	What's All The Fuss About A Launch?	Page 8
2	Developing A Solid Launch Strategy	Page 9
3	When Is The Right Time To Plan A Launch?	Page 13
4	Make It Happen!	Page 20

1 WHAT'S ALL THE FUSS ABOUT A LAUNCH?

About a year ago we shared our insights on how to write a strong business plan and better understand your business in our book, the *Start Smart Business Plan Guide*. The book incorporated many of the lessons that we had learned as first time entrepreneurs about competition, pricing, marketing, financial planning and market research.

In this book we plan to dissect another important part of the entrepreneurial journey, successfully launching a business, product or service. It took us three years to get to a point where we were ready to launch, and depending on the nature of your business and market it may take you more or less time. Regardless of how long it takes for you to launch, it is an important milestone in the life of your business. As a result it is important to devote the time and resource necessary to making it successful.

In the following chapters we'll discuss how to:

- Develop a Robust Launch Strategy
- Determine the Appropriate Time to Plan a Launch
- Put Your Plan into Action

2 DEVELOPING A SOLID LAUNCH STRATEGY

We've all seen successful launches. Whether it's an in-person or online affair, the final product often makes it seem like the process is simple and straightforward. Develop a product/service, send out a few emails and then you've launched. This perspective, however, couldn't be further from the truth.

Product launches just like business ideas require research, knowledge and the convening of a skilled and knowledgeable marketing team. If you're part of a small business it may mean relying on the skills you collectively have. Regardless, the goal should be to develop a clear understanding of your value proposition and how best to engage with your target audience. In today's market in particular, savvy consumers demand products that create value across a number of dimensions including quality, price, customer service experience and flexibility in functions. To ensure that you are able to meet these expectations, it is important to develop a strong launch strategy.

A well-defined launch strategy serves as a living document to provide accountability and traceability throughout the launch process. Below are a few key components:

A. Purpose

The most important part of your launch strategy is the purpose. What do you hope to achieve from the launch and which metrics do you plan to use to measure success? Launches are meant to provide an opportunity to create visibility and brand recognition for businesses, which ultimately fuels growth. Through the increased exposure that they create, launches expand your customer base and create the potential for increased sales volume and revenue. The expanded customer base can come from increasing opportunities to engage with existing customers, and/or identifying and engaging with new customers.

B. Checkpoints

Once the purpose and metrics for determining success (post launch) have been defined, it is important to set-up regular checkpoints to ensure that you are on track both for the planned launch event and for the development of the product/service that you plan to launch. Even in instances where the product or service has already been developed and some customers have been acquired, it is important to continuously conduct quality assessment tests, and incorporate feedback received to ensure that you're putting "your best foot forward". This should come in the form of regular meetings with your team and other important individuals. It may be helpful to develop tools for documenting tasks, progress and critical issues. Examples are shown in Figures 1 and 2. The sample checklist in Figure 3 contains some of the milestones around which the timeline and status documents can be developed.

Phase I: Pre-Launch Planning 6 - 8 weeks	Phase II: Mid-Launch 2 – 4 weeks	Phase III: Post Launch Indefinite
Cross - Phase: Build Awareness & Conduct Quality Assessment		
Pre-Launch Objectives & Activities:	Mid-Launch Objectives & Activities:	Post Launch Planning Objectives & Activities:

Figure 1 – Sample Launch Timeline

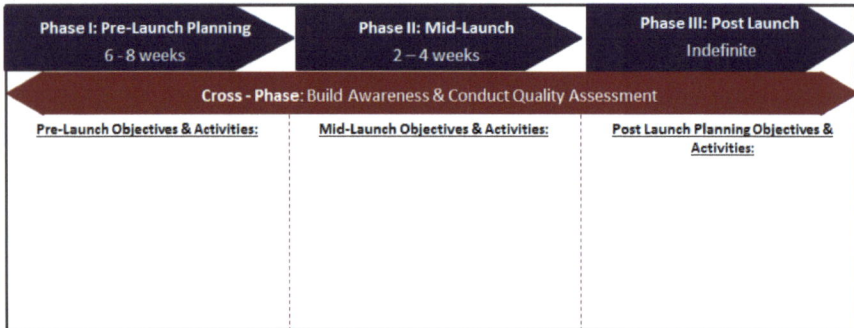

Figure 2 – Sample Status Report

Stage	Principle	Do You Have This	
		Yes	No
Launch Planning	Decide on your goals for the event and ways to hold yourself accountable		
Pre-Launch	Create a communications plan to announce the launch via multiple channels		
Mid-Launch	Implement a continuous quality assessment and review process for your product, and any materials that you plan to distribute at your launch event		
Post Launch	Take advantage of the increased visibility to draw attention to your brand by implementing your post-launch strategy		

Figure 3 - Sample Launch Checklist

C. Team/Key Stakeholders

Ideally a launch should not be a one man or woman show. There should be clearly defined activities tied to the objectives and the checkpoints discussed above, and for each of these a clear task owner should be assigned (e.g., in Figure 2 this is the field labeled task owner). Whether the individual completes the task on their own or solicits the help of others they become responsible for it, ensuring that no important elements are overlooked.

D. Putting Your Strategy into Action

Once you've defined your strategy, it is important to determine the appropriate timing, logistical, and publicity requirements related to your launch. The next chapter goes into more detail on the timing of a launch and how best to go about putting your strategy into action.

E. Contingencies

Unfortunately things can go wrong, even when a solid launch strategy and implementation plan are in place. While it isn't possible to plan for every unfortunate circumstance, it is important to stay alert and increase the chances of catching mistakes early, in order to correct them and minimize any potentially negative effects.

F. Post Launch Agenda

Once you've put the time, effort and money into ensuring a successful launch, it is important to plan towards sustaining the energy and momentum generated to create additional sales opportunities. Ideally the post launch agenda should include:

- Post-Launch Publicity Campaigns- Identify the appropriate channels and messaging to keep you on your existing and prospective customer's radar
- Customer Incentive Schemes- Determine strategies to develop customer loyalty raw in customers while maintaining profitability
- Narratives of Your Brand and History- Create your "5-minute elevator pitch", which concisely describes who you are, what you have to offer and why customers should choose you
- Documentation of Challenges Faced and Lessons Learned: Create a list of challenges and lessons to ensure that you remain alert and responsive to change

3 WHEN IS THE RIGHT TIME TO PLAN A LAUNCH?

A. Understanding Your Options

Markets are not static they are subject to volatility and fluctuations; therefore, when attempting to launch a new product or service it is imperative that you understand how narrow or wide the "window of opportunity" is for success. The general consensus on the timing of launches is that releasing a product prematurely can mean encountering a lack of adequate consumer demand, while waiting too long can result in an excess of competition with more well-established brands. The timing of your launch can literally make the difference between a flourishing new product and a quickly forgotten one. It is therefore crucial to develop an understanding of:

- Your Environment- Who are your competitors and what are the relevant factors affecting your market?
- Your Potential Customers- Who are you targeting and how will you reach them?
- The Benefits and Challenges of the Time Frame You Have Chosen- What are the pros and cons of your chosen launch timeframe?

In the table on the next page, fill in details on each of these three factors for your business.

Your Environment	
Your Potential Customers	
Benefits of Chosen Launch Timing	Challenges Created by Chosen Launch Timing

Figure 4 - Developing an Understanding of Your Proposed Launch Timing

B. What the Experts Say

According to a recent study published in *Entrepreneurship Theory and Practice*[1],

"The optimal time of entry depends on the hostility of the learning environment since it has an impact on dimensions of performance, such as profit potential and mortality risk."

What this quote and the study suggest, are that some element of delay in a launch strategy can be beneficial. The key, however, is to understand how long to wait and in which type of markets waiting even makes sense. Going back to our fictitious company Killer Heels from the *Start Smart Business Plan Guide*, we'll explore the impact of different environments on launch timing.

---

[1] Levesque, Moren, Maria Minniti, and Dean Shepard. "Entrepreneurs' Decisions on Timing of Entry: Learning from Participation and From the Experience of Others." *Entrepreneurship Theory and Practice* Vol. 33 Issue 2 (2009): 547-70. Print.

Using the *Start Smart Business Plan Guide*, Killer Heels has spent the last six months conducting research and compiling the information needed to develop a strong business plan. With a well-defined strategy and an innovative product (i.e. convertible stiletto heels which allow wearers to switch between flats and stilettos), Killer Heels is now ready to launch. Their plan is to invite potential customers to a local hotel, where they've rented out a room for their event. The team, however, is confused about the best timing for it.

Assuming that the overall economic climate is fairly stable, let's consider two potential scenarios for the company:

- **Scenario One** – There are currently no competitors in the market, and Killer Heels has the necessary intellectual property rights in place (i.e. patents and copyrights) to protect its products and ideas.
- **Scenario Two** – While there are currently no competitors in the market, Killer Heels has heard that another start-up with a similar product, called Stylin' Divas, is in the process of launching their brand. In this scenario it is correct to assume that Killer Heels has not taken advantage of its intellectual property rights (i.e. there are no patents or copyrights in place).

What should they do in each of the scenarios? You'll notice that the biggest difference between the two is intellectual property. Having intellectual property for their product creates a clear competitive advantage, by reducing the risk of duplication and therefore the chances that competitors can create a product which existing and potential customers will view as a substitute. As you've probably guessed in **Scenario One**, Killer Heels can delay its launch while in **Scenario Two**; this may not be the best idea.

More broadly speaking, any situation in which you have a distinct and protected advantage over existing or potential competitors creates more flexibility for the timing of your launch. Do you have a distinct and protected advantage over current or future competitors? Alternatively do you have weaknesses that make you particularly vulnerable with respect to launch timing? Write them out on the next page.

Start Smart

C. Leveraging the Internet to Support Your Product Launch

Prior to the advent of the internet, publicizing a product launch meant having a significant advertising budget to spread the word via print, radio and or television. While this still holds true in some instances, the rapid growth of the internet (i.e. both in terms of content and accessibility) has created a more far reaching and low cost alternative to engaging with current and potential customers. Consumers now garner information from a variety of sources (e.g., blogs, Facebook, Twitter, Instagram etc.), thus a successful launch requires an understanding of these tools and how they can be used. Below are suggestions on how the internet can help you generate the publicity required for a successful launch.

- **Search Engine Optimization (SEO)**

Prior to beginning your online outreach, it is important to have a "home base" such as a search-friendly website or blog that people can refer to in order to seek more information, ask a question or if possible make a purchase. Your website or blog should include a number of elements including:
   - Appropriate coding to facilitate searches
   - Keyword-rich content to ensure that the page appears in relevant searches
   - Title tags and header text to make it easier to recognize
   - A unique URL
   - Meta information that succinctly describes your new product or service to improve its appearance in searches

- **E-mail Marketing**

Email is an inexpensive way to engage with your target audience, in a manner that typically allows you to share as much or as little as you deem relevant. It can also create the opportunity for you to be more selective in the information that is being delivered (e.g., sharing information on sales and promotions with selected customers). The key to successful email marketing, however, is not just sending an email but instead sharing the right information with the right people. Great tools for managing email marketing include traditional email servers and newer mass marketing tools such as Mailchimp. The overall goal of email campaigns is to keep your product or service "top of mind" for your current and future customers.

- **Social Media Marketing**

Whether it's through a free Facebook page or (paid) promoted posts and tweets, social media presents a tremendous opportunity to engage with your audience. The key to being successful in the social media space, is creating a community where your "followers/fans" can learn more about your product/service, and identifying/encouraging brand champions (i.e. people with a strong online presence that are willing to serve as evangelists for your brand). It is also important to understand which members of your audience are active on the various social media platforms, a quick Google search can provide you with the most up to date figures.

- **Cross – Platform Promotion**

In addition to your company's website, blog and/or social media profiles, it can also be helpful to take advantage of the power of your network. Use your existing relationships or develop new ones to help you identify well-respected websites that are willing to give you some real estate on theirs. This may be through purchasing space for an ad or requesting an "honorable mention".

- **Traditional Methods**

While online advertising seems to have garnered significant popularity, in some instances traditional television, print or radio media outreach still remains an effective way to create visibility for your brand.

Regardless of which method you choose to draw attention to your products and services, it is important to share information which is actually "newsworthy". You should be able to clearly convey:

- o Who you are
- o What you have to offer
- o How your product/service differs from the competition or your existing product lines
- o Why customers should care
- o How they can find you

Outline your internet marketing plan on the next page.

Start Smart

4 MAKE IT HAPPEN!

Now that you've armed yourself with a solid strategy for launching, the next step is the actual launch. Enjoy the event, stay vigilant and most importantly look forward to the success ahead.

It is important to remember, however, to not let all of your effort go to waste. In the table below write down the goals that you set in planning the product launch and think about where you did well and where you would like to improve.

Goal	Successes	Areas for Improvement

Figure 5 - Launch Learnings

Now you're ready to launch, all the best!

Start Smart

Notes

Start Smart

Notes

Start Smart

Notes

About the Author

 Start Smart was founded by Juliana A. Taylor in 2011 to empower African entrepreneurs, through the provision of business and financial literacy tools. She has a strong interest in entrepreneurship and looks forward to contributing towards the development of African businesses.

Juliana holds a BA in Economics from Princeton University and a Masters in Management Studies from Duke University's Fuqua School of Business. She has also spent time working for Google in Ghana on its business and university outreach initiatives, and Accenture in Washington, D.C. as a consultant for federal, private sector and nonprofit clients.

Start Smart

www.ingramcontent.com/pod-product-compliance
Lightning Source LLC
Chambersburg PA
CBHW041622180526
45159CB00002BC/977